The **Sophia Day**® Creative Team-
Kayla Pearson, Timothy Zowada,
Stephanie Strouse, Megan Johnson, Mel Sauder

Designed by Stephanie Strouse

Published and Distributed by MVP Kids Media, LLC
Mesa, Arizona, USA
Printed by RR Donnelley Asia Printing Solutions, Ltd
Dongguan City, Guangdong Province, China
DOM Oct 2018, Job # 03-006-01

help**me**
B E C O M E™

Becoming *a Friend*
& Overcoming **Being a Bully**™

REAL
mvpkids®

STOP BULLYING
™
S.T.A.N.D.
a 3-part series

ST**AND** Down, Bullies™

SOPHIA DAY®

Written by Kayla Pearson   *Illustrated by* Timothy Zowada

TABLE OF CONTENTS

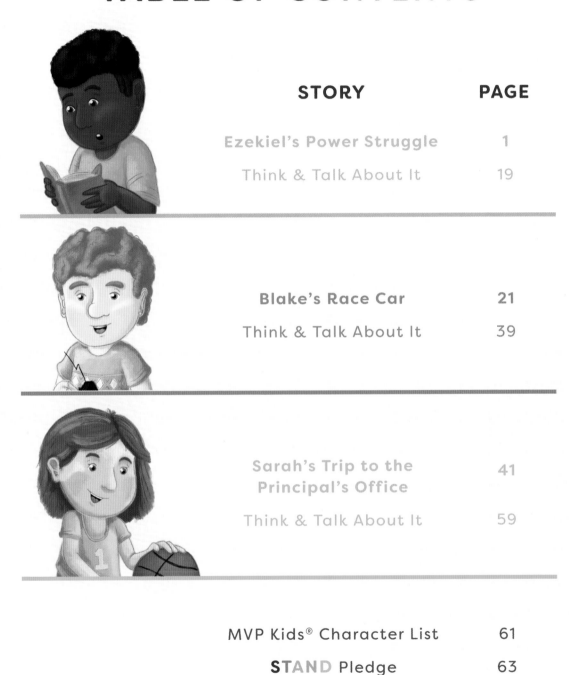

Ezekiel's Power Struggle

Ezekiel was playing football with his friends at the park. "Touch down!" yelled Ezekiel as his team scored.

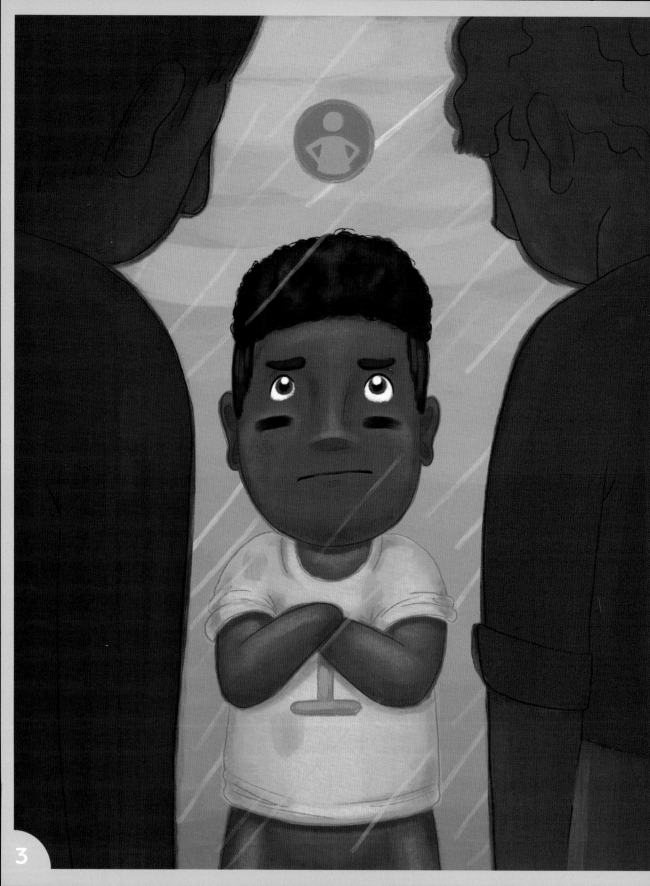

A group of older kids often picked on Ezekiel and his friends. They told Ezekiel and his friends to leave the field. Ezekiel tried to **stand up to them**, but one of the kids pushed him.

"If you don't leave now, someone is going to get hurt." The kids were much bigger. There was nothing Ezekiel and his friends could do.

Ezekiel hated feeling so *powerless.*

6

The next day at book club,
Ezekiel told a boy he was too
little to be in their group.
He even pushed him down!

The leader saw what happened
and sent Ezekiel home.

That night, Ezekiel and his mom talked about what happened. He explained how frustrated and powerless he felt at the park. Ezekiel told her he wanted to feel powerful and that's why he acted the way he did at school.

"Ezekiel, I'm sorry that happened to you yesterday. You were angry because it was not right for them to kick you off the field. Next time, come to me and I will help. When you don't deal with these issues right away, they **build up inside you** until you take it out on someone else."

13

"No matter how others treat you, **bullying is NEVER acceptable.** If you want to be powerful, be kind. It takes more strength to be kind than it does to be mean. When you bully others, the hurt and pain is spread to someone else. I know it can be hard, but you need to take a **STAND**."

"What would your dad say if he were here?" asked his mom.

Ezekiel thought about his dad who was serving in the military.

15

Ezekiel missed his dad and knew what he would say.

 " **S**tand tall and be confident.

 **T**ell an adult if you run into trouble.

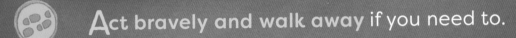 **A**ct bravely and walk away if you need to.

Notice what is going on around you.

Display kindness to others."

16

The next week at book club, Ezekiel apologized to the boy. He displayed kindness by welcoming him into his group. From now on, Ezekiel was going to take a **STAND** against bullying.

THINK & TALK ABOUT IT

Ezekiel's Power Struggle

Discuss the story...

1. What was Ezekiel doing at the park?

2. When the older children bullied Ezekiel, how did that make him feel?

3. Where did Ezekiel go the next day? What happened there?

4. What did Ezekiel's mom say about bullying?

5. What ways did Ezekiel **STAND** against bullying?

 **Stand Confident**    **Tell an Adult**   **Act Bravely & Walk Away**   **Notice Surroundings**    **Display Kindness**

Discuss how to apply the story...

1. What do you think Ezekiel should have done differently?

2. Has there been a time when you bullied someone else? What happened?

3. How did it make you feel? How do you think it made the other person feel?

4. What could you do to make things right between you and that person?

5. How can you display kindness to others this week?

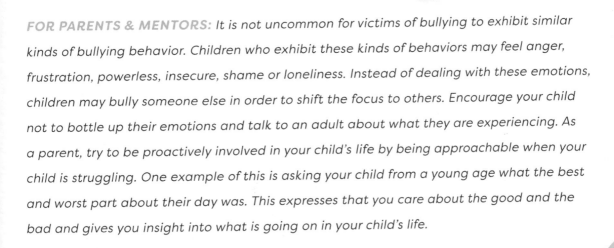

FOR PARENTS & MENTORS: *It is not uncommon for victims of bullying to exhibit similar kinds of bullying behavior. Children who exhibit these kinds of behaviors may feel anger, frustration, powerless, insecure, shame or loneliness. Instead of dealing with these emotions, children may bully someone else in order to shift the focus to others. Encourage your child not to bottle up their emotions and talk to an adult about what they are experiencing. As a parent, try to be proactively involved in your child's life by being approachable when your child is struggling. One example of this is asking your child from a young age what the best and worst part about their day was. This expresses that you care about the good and the bad and gives you insight into what is going on in your child's life.*

Blake's Race Car

School was out and summer break had begun!
Blake was excited
to get started on
his list for summer break.

As Blake worked on his summer list,
it seemed like his little sister was
always getting in the way.

Blake became frustrated.
He wanted to do things *his way.*

He let his frustration build up and began to pick on Annie. Blake took her toys and made fun of her. He didn't realize how selfish he was becoming.

One day, Leo came over to race remote control cars with Blake. Annie wanted to join, but Blake wouldn't let her.

Trying to impress Leo, Blake made a mean joke about Annie. Annie was hurt by his words and **walked away.**

Blake laughed as she walked away, but Leo wasn't laughing.

"That wasn't funny, Blake. **That was mean.** We could have let her join us," said Leo, **standing up** to Blake.

Blake tried to ignore him and kept racing his car. "It wasn't that mean," Blake thought. "Was it?"

"Blaaaaaaake!"
his mom called a few
minutes later.

Blake stopped racing and
walked back to the house.

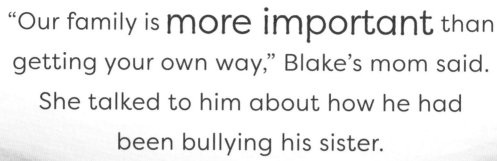

"Our family is **more important** than getting your own way," Blake's mom said. She talked to him about how he had been bullying his sister.

Then, Blake's mom helped him think through ways to include his sister. She also explained ways he could kindly communicate that he needed his own space.

Blake walked over to Annie who was crying. He felt ashamed about how he had treated her. **"I'm sorry** I was being selfish. You are more important than getting my own way," Blake said.

To **display kindness** to his sister, Blake invited Annie to race cars with them. They created an obstacle course and enjoyed racing cars all afternoon. Including Annie turned out to be fun for everyone!

THINK & TALK ABOUT IT

Discuss the story...

1. What was Blake excited about at the beginning of the story?

2. How did Blake feel when his sister got in his way?

3. What did Blake start to do to his sister?

4. What did Blake's mom say was more important than Blake getting his own way?

5. What ways did you see Blake and Leo **STAND** against bullying?

 **Stand Confident**　 **Tell an Adult**　 **Act Bravely & Walk Away**　 **Notice Surroundings**　 **Display Kindness**

Discuss how to apply the story...

1. How does it make you feel when your brothers or sisters get in your way?

2. What do you do when they get in your way?

3. What could you do differently in the future?

4. Why do you think family members are more important than doing things your way?

5. What ways can you display kindness to your family this week?

FOR PARENTS & MENTORS: *Sibling arguing is a typical occurrence, and parents can encourage their children to try to work it out on their own. However, sibling arguing can cross the line into bullying. Be aware of the following warning signs: unequal balance of power, consistent patterns, no empathy toward the other sibling and no reconciliation after the conflict. Sibling bullying is just as damaging as peer bullying and should be taken seriously. Be sure to create a safe environment at home where any form of bullying is unacceptable. Encourage empathy and respect, disciplining bullying behavior immediately. Coach your children in healthy ways to deal with conflict to create a safe and peaceful home.*

*For additional tips and reference information, visit **www.realMVPkids.com**.*

Sarah's Trip to the Principal's Office

Sarah sat in the principal's office.
She *couldn't believe* she was
in trouble for *bullying*.

It started at school. Sarah enjoyed playing basketball with a girl named Amber, but Amber was mean to others. Sarah didn't like it when Amber treated others badly.

Sarah was *afraid* that if she told Amber to stop, Amber would pick on her, too.

After a while, Amber pressured Sarah into teasing others. One day, a teacher overheard Amber and Sarah bullying another student in the hallway.

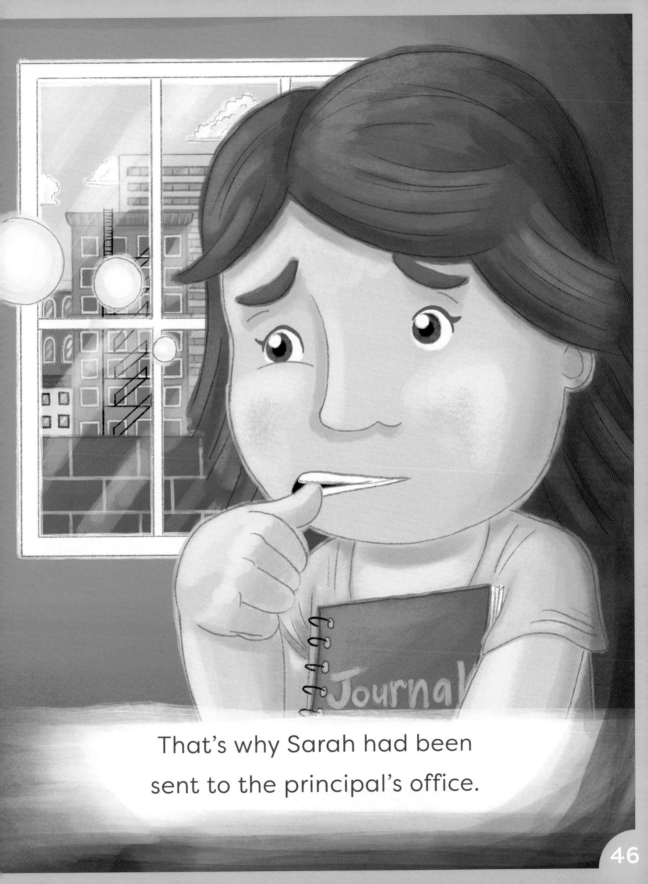

That's why Sarah had been sent to the principal's office.

That night Sarah's mom talked to her about bullying. "Sarah, you know better than to be mean to others. We are supposed to **stand up** for those who are weak and beaten down."
Sarah *did* know better.
She didn't want to be a bully.

The next day, Sarah decided to **stand tall and be confident** when she saw Amber.

She told Amber that she didn't want to play together if she was going to be **mean to others.**

49

Amber didn't like Sarah standing up to her. Just as Sarah feared, Amber began to make fun of Sarah as well.

Sarah acted bravely and walked away.

A couple days later, Sarah noticed Amber yelling at a boy on the playground. Sarah immediately **told the teacher** on recess duty.

Amber glared at Sarah as the teacher led her to the principal's office.

After school, Sarah **told her mom** what happened. Her mom was proud of her for taking a **STAND** against bullying. She also gave her a new challenge.

"You know, Amber might be feeling sad, angry or alone. Is there anything you could do to **display kindness** to her?" Sarah's mom asked.

Sarah thought all night about what she could do.

Sarah tried different ways to **display kindness** toward Amber. Each time Sarah was kind, she saw a change in Amber. Sarah talked to her mom about inviting Amber over to play. Their whole family could show kindness!

"Thanks, Sarah, for being so kind to me," Amber told her after dinner.

"I'm glad we're friends again.
Let's always be kind to others!"
Sarah answered.

THINK & TALK ABOUT IT

Sarah's Trip to the Principal's Office

Discuss the story...

1. What did Sarah like to do with Amber at school?

2. Why was Sarah afraid to ask Amber to stop being mean to others?

3. Why was Sarah sent to the principal's office?

4. How did Sarah's mom challenge Sarah to act toward Amber?

5. What ways did Sarah **STAND** against bullying?

 **Stand Confident**   **Tell an Adult**   **Act Bravely & Walk Away**   **Notice Surroundings**    **Display Kindness**

For additional tips and reference information, visit www.realMVPkids.com.

Discuss how to apply the story...

1. Has there been a time when you joined a friend who was bullying someone else and became a bully, too? What happened?

2. What should you do if your friends are bullying someone else?

3. Even though Amber was mean to Sarah, Sarah still displayed kindness. Do you think you could do that? Why or why not?

4. If you bullied someone in the past, do you think you could change and **STAND** against bullying in the future?

5. How are you going to **STAND** against bullying now?

FOR PARENTS & MENTORS: Any child is capable of exhibiting bullying behavior. Studies show 30% of school age children admitted to bullying others. If your child is sent home for bullying, do not overreact, but take it seriously. Listen to your child's side of the story and calmly express why bullying behavior is not acceptable. Discuss with your child different ways to handle a situation like that in the future. Encourage your child to apologize and display kindness to the hurt person. It may take some time to help correct your child's behavior, but remember to acknowledge positive efforts from your child. Remind your child that it's the bullying behavior you dislike, but you still love your child. If the bullying behavior continues to be an issue, reach out to teachers and counselors for help.

Meet the
mvpkids

featured in
STAND Down, Bullies™
with their families

EZEKIEL JORDAN

MRS. JASMINE JORDAN
"Mom"

MR. DARIUS JORDAN
"Dad"

FRANKIE RUSSO

BLAKE JAMES

MRS. HANNAH
JAMES
"Mom"

ANNIE JAMES

SARAH COHEN-GOLDSTEIN

MRS. ESTER
GOLDSTEIN
"Mom"

LEO RUSSO

JULIA ROJAS

MIRIAM NASSER

mvpkids®

STAND against bullying!

Will YOU take a STAND to stop bullying?

Stand in front of a mirror and say the pledge aloud, then share with someone how you've decided to STAND against bullying.

Use this QR code for a download of the STAND pledge to sign and display!

I pledge to take a

S.T.A.N.D.

when faced with any bullying situation.

I promise that I will strive to...

 Stand tall and be confident.

 Tell an adult if I run into trouble.

 Act bravely and walk away if I need to.

 Notice what is going on around me.

 Display kindness to others.

In a study conducted by StopBullying.gov, "about 49% of children in grades 4–12 reported being bullied by other students at school at least once during the past month, whereas 30.8% reported bullying others during that time."[1] From a very young age, we need to help our children understand and STAND against bullying.

———————

Do you need more resources and help regarding bullying? Please visit our website at

www.realMVPkids.com/stand-against-bullying/

The U.S. official government website can be found at

www.stopbullying.gov/

[1] *"Facts About Bullying." StopBullying.gov, www.stopbullying.gov/media/facts/index.html.*

YONG
CHEN

LEO
RUSSO

FRANKIE
RUSSO

JULIA
ROJAS

GABBY
GONZALEZ

ANNIE
JAMES

AANYA
PATEL

BLAKE
JAMES

SARAH
COHEN-
GOLDSTEIN